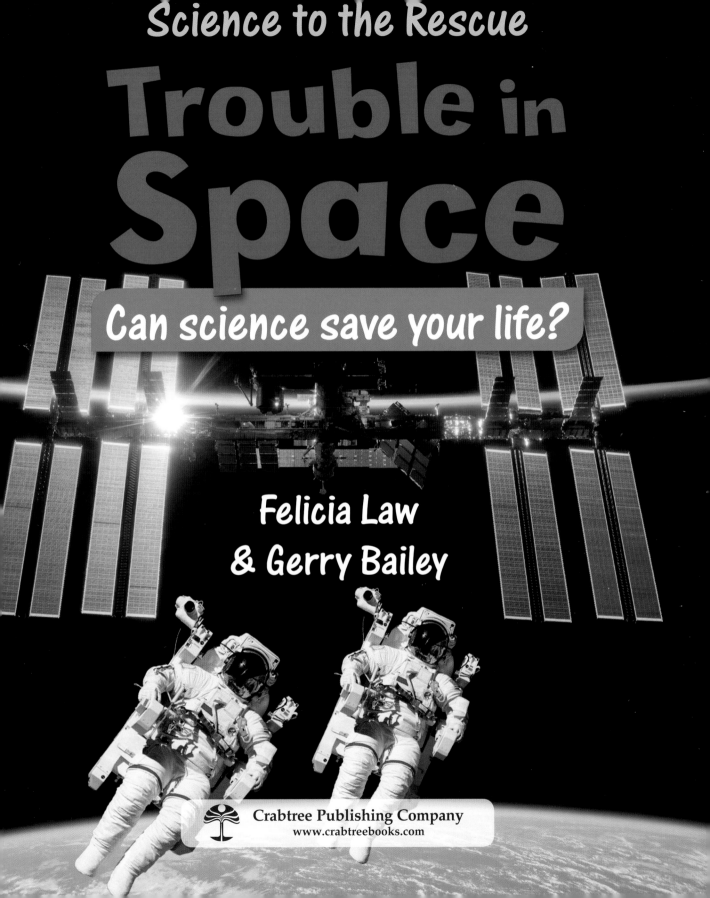

Science to the Rescue

Trouble in Space

Can science save your life?

Felicia Law
& Gerry Bailey

Crabtree Publishing Company
www.crabtreebooks.com

Crabtree Publishing Company
www.crabtreebooks.com
1-800-387-7650

PMB 59051, 350 Fifth Ave.
59th Floor,
New York, NY 10118

616 Welland Ave.
St. Catharines, ON
L2M 5V6

Published by Crabtree Publishing in 2016

Author: Felicia Law and Gerry Bailey

Illustrator: Leighton Noyes

Editors: Shirley Duke, Crystal Sikkens

Proofreader: Wendy Scavuzzo

**Production coordinator and
  Prepress technician:** Tammy McGarr

Print coordinator: Margaret Amy Salter

Printed in Canada/102015/IH20150821

Photographs:
Cover
main picture; 3Dsculptor / shutterstock
middle; MarcelClemens / shutterstock
bottom; NASA

Shutterstock: p1- NikoNomad (NASA); p7 top left
- Ali Ender Birer; p12 - Pavel L Photo and Video
/ shutterstock.com; p13 left - vicspacewalker /
shutterstock.com; p15 middle - vicspacewalker /
shutterstock.com; p17 right - Naeblys; p25 main -
MarcelClemens

Nasa photos: p2 ; p6; p7 bottom right; p8 all; p13
right; p14 bottom; p14-15 main; p16-17; p18;
p19 all photos; p22; p23 all photos; p25 bottom;
p26 top; 26 bottom; p27 top left; top right; center
right; center left; bottom left; p28 bottom left,
center and right

Other photos: p26 middle - Crew of Soyuz T-13.

Library and Archives Canada Cataloguing in Publication

Law, Felicia, author
　　Trouble in space / Felicia Law, Gerry Bailey.

(Science to the rescue)
Illustrator: Leighton Noyes.
Includes index.
Issued in print and electronic formats.
ISBN 978-0-7787-1676-1 (bound).--
ISBN 978-0-7787-1683-9 (paperback).--
ISBN 978-1-4271-7674-5 (pdf).--ISBN 978-1-4271-7670-7 (html)

　　1. Outer space--Exploration--Juvenile literature. 2. International
Space Station--Juvenile literature. 3. Solar system--Juvenile literature.
I. Bailey, Gerry, 1945-, author II. Noyes, Leighton, illustrator III. Title.
IV. Series: Science to the rescue (St. Catharines, Ont.)

QB501.3.L385 2015　　　　j523.2　　　C2015-903232-6
　　　　　　　　　　　　　　　　　　　　　　C2015-903233-4

Library of Congress Cataloging-in-Publication Data

Law, Felicia, author.
　Trouble in space / Felicia Law, Gerry Bailey ;
illustrated by Leighton Noyes.
　　　pages cm. -- (Science to the rescue)
　Includes index.
　ISBN 978-0-7787-1676-1 (reinforced library binding : alk. paper) --
ISBN 978-0-7787-1683-9 (pbk. : alk. paper) --
ISBN 978-1-4271-7674-5 (electronic pdf : alk. paper) --
ISBN 978-1-4271-7670-7 (electronic html : alk. paper)
1. International Space Station--Juvenile literature. 2. Space flight--
Juvenile literature. 3. Survival--Juvenile literature. 4. Outer space-
-Exploration--Juvenile literature. I. Bailey, Gerry, 1945- author. II.
Noyes, Leighton, illustrator. III. Title.

TL793.L2975 2016
　629.4'1--dc23

　　　　　　　　　　　　　　　　　　　2015030124

Contents

Joe and Dr. Bea's story

Hi! My name is Joe. Dr. Bea and I have just returned from another adventure. This time it happened in space! Yes—248 miles (400 km) up there above your heads! Normal planes fly 7.5 miles (12 km) above the ground, so imagine how much higher we were!

This was our most exciting adventure ever! We have been carrying out experiments on the International Space Station, or the ISS for short. Yes—we have been LIVING in space!

So, let me tell you all about it...

It was Day One! Dr. Bea and I arrived at the Johnson Space Center in Houston, Texas. It is the home of Mission Control—the place where **NASA** guides the International Space Station operations. It was going to be our home, too—for a while ...

... as we began our training to become astronauts.

The ISS

The International Space Station, is a laboratory in space. It is speeding around and around Earth on a circular path, or orbit, about **248 miles (400 km)** above us.

High speed

It is going so fast, it only takes 90 minutes to make one orbit. In fact, it's flying at 8 miles (7.7 km) a second. That's fast enough to go to the Moon and back in about a day!

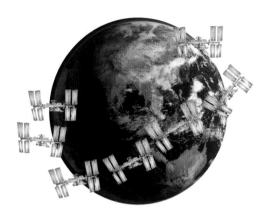

Who's on board?

The space station has made it possible for people to live and work in space. In fact, humans have been living in space every day since the first crew arrived in 1989.

During an orbit, the crew are in daylight for about 45 minutes and darkness for another 45 minutes. They see the Sun rise and set 16 times a day.

Each new crew starts a new ISS expedition, which usually lasts about six months. There are normally six crew members on board at any time, coming from the United States, Russia, Japan, Canada, and Europe.

What are they doing up there?

NASA and other space agencies throughout the world are all working on a plan to explore other worlds. The space station is one of the first steps. Up there, scientists are developing new technologies and conducting experiments that could not be done on Earth. The ISS is also an observatory where they can observe and take photos of Earth, the solar system, and other parts of the universe.

An ISS photograph shows the Sarychev volcano near Japan as it erupts, pouring ash and steam into the sky.

Piece by piece

The ISS is an ever-changing and ever-increasing collection of pressurized parts called **modules**. It has a connecting **truss**, or support, structure that runs from one end of the ISS to the other. Connecting modules called **nodes** are used to attach pieces of the space station to each other.

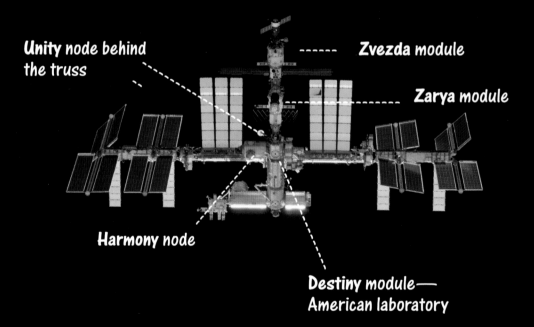

Unity node behind the truss

Zvezda module

Zarya module

Harmony node

Destiny module— American laboratory

A robotic arm called Canadarm2 is attached outside the ISS. It helped build the ISS. It can also be used to move astronauts around and help dock visiting spacecraft.

The first part of the ISS was launched by the Russians on November 20, 1998. This Russian module is named **Zarya**. The first crew arrived two years later.

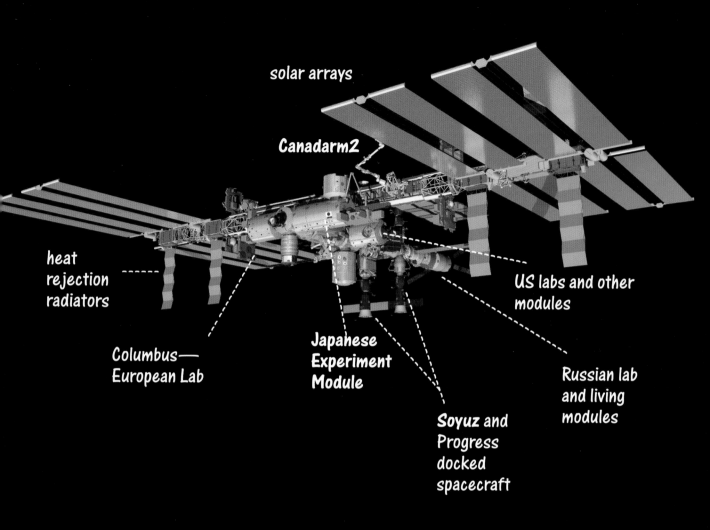

solar arrays

Canadarm2

heat
rejection
radiators

Columbus—
European Lab

Japanese
Experiment
Module

US labs and other
modules

Russian lab
and living
modules

Soyuz and
Progress
docked
spacecraft

The first modules contained parts to make the ISS work. These modules were also where the astronauts lived.

The ISS gets power from the Sun by using 16 solar arrays mounted on the truss. They have a wingspan of 240 feet (73 m), which is wider than a Boeing 777. The lab, or laboratory, modules are where astronauts do their research.

Wearing a space suit

To work outside the space station, Dr. Bea and I would need the protection of a spacesuit.

After putting on special underwear, the astronaut puts on an undersuit that contains tubes of cold water for cooling the body.

The cap under the helmet has a radio for communication.

The outer suit is made of two parts that are buttoned together.

They are the bottom...

... and the rigid, or stiff, top that carries the backpack and control module.

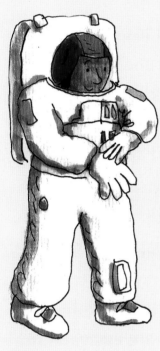

The gloves must fit well and be flexible to hold small objects.

The helmet protects against the Sun's glare and other harmful rays.

The backpack is the life support system. It provides oxygen to breathe, and removes carbon dioxide and moisture.

A display and control module acts as a mini workstation.

The outlet for the liquid cooling and ventilation undersuit.

Tough boots

Training

Once a person has been selected to be an astronaut **candidate,** the training begins. It can take two to three years to be fully qualified. After the initial training period, these new astronauts will support astronauts who are already in space. Then, they wait—sometimes for years—until the day they are assigned to a space flight.

Dr. Bea and I spent a lot of time underwater in a huge pool. Swimming in water is similar to being in space, but not quite the same. You're not truly weightless like in space, but you're what is called neutrally buoyant. This means you don't float to the surface or sink to the bottom.

We also had lessons in Russian and Japanese. Our training included learning how to use the modules that had been added to the space station by Europe and Japan.

Astronauts work in the huge pool at the Neutral Buoyancy Laboratory to practice how to use their spacesuits.

Training involves learning about basic space station systems and routines.

Astronauts need to learn how to do tasks outside the space station, so they are able to fix anything that might break.

Learning to float

Before astronauts can go into space, they must experience weightlessness. This can be done in a large pool, such as the one in the Neutral Buoyancy Laboratory at the Johnson Space Center in Houston, Texas. The water tank is 203 feet (62 m) long, 102 feet (31 m) wide, and 40 feet (12 m) deep. At the bottom sits a model of the ISS, which is the same size as the one orbiting Earth. That's why the tank needs to be so big.

Speaking Russian

The ISS is a joint project between the United States and Russia. Training astronauts make many trips between NASA and the Gagarin Cosmonaut Training Center in Star City, just outside Moscow, Russia. Astronauts must be able to understand Russian, so they can talk with the Russian Mission Control Center and understand their Russian instructors.

Bea and I crammed into the Russian Soyuz spacecraft. When the first engines lit, there was a loud rumbling and things started to shake.

Then the main engines lit, and we built up speed. There was one bang after another, as parts of the rocket were jettisoned, or dropped.

And just like that, we were in space.

Getting there

Astronauts are launched into space aboard a Russian Soyuz spacecraft. It blasts off from the Baikonur Cosmodrome in Kazakhstan. The cramped capsule they travel in is part of a five-stage rocket. However, four of these parts will be jettisoned early in the flight. The flight usually takes 50 hours because of the complicated maneuvers needed to meet the orbiting ISS. As the craft approaches, the Soyuz uses radar that can detect the ISS from 124 miles (200 km) away and will help it to dock automatically—and precisely.

The stages of the rocket will fire one after the other to get the rocket from 0 to 17,400 miles per hour (28,000 kph) in just eight and a half minutes.

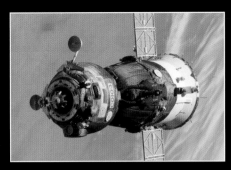

The Soyuz *TMA-6* spacecraft launched on April 15, 2005. It held three crew members.

Astronauts practice launching in a **simulator** that copies the noise and shaking of a launch.

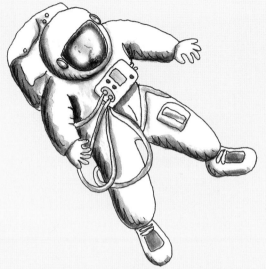

We are
lucky
we have
gravity
on Earth.

Without it, we'd all go floating off into space. Dr. Bea and I had to learn to move around without it.

Aboard the space station, everything would seem weightless. This means that everything that isn't fastened down can float around— including people.

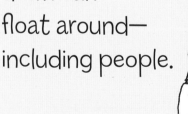

Gravity

Gravity is the force that pulls an object toward another. It pulls us towards the center of gravity—which is the center of Earth. Gravity gives us weight. So the farther you go from the center of Earth, the less pull—and the less weight—you experience.

A special plane lets astronauts feel the sensations of microgravity for around 20-25 seconds. They sometimes vomit, giving the plane the nickname "Vomit Comet," but it is also called the "Weightless Wonder."

Microgravity

Aboard the ISS, the astronauts live in an environment of **microgravity**, which makes things seem weightless. At an orbit height of 200–250 miles (322–402 km), Earth's gravity is still strong. So, the reason things float in the ISS is because of **freefall**.

Freefall

Freefall means falling back toward Earth, or in this case, falling around it. If you throw a ball up, it moves upward, then curves, and then gravity pulls it back to the ground. If you were to let go of a ball at the start of a freefall ride at an amusement park, you and the ball would fall at the same speed. It would seem as though the ball is floating in front of you. This is what happens on the ISS. Gravity is pulling the ISS, the astronauts, and the objects on board toward Earth. Since they are all falling at the same speed, the astronauts and objects appear to float.

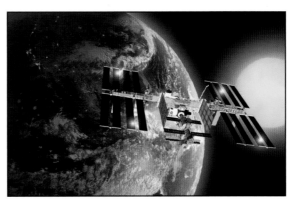

Gravity is pulling the ISS toward Earth, but it never hits the planet. This is because the ISS is moving so fast that it matches the curve of Earth. Therefore, the ISS falls around Earth instead.

After our capsule reached the module, the docking took place. We climbed through the tiny airlock and entered the Zarya module. Bea and I had to take a moment to get used to the weightlessness. Then we headed down a circular tunnel and into the Harmony node.

The rest of the crew was there to greet us—with our dinner trays!

The crew

The crew usually works ten hours per day Monday to Friday, and five hours on Saturdays. The rest of the time is their own to relax or catch up on work.

Daily schedule:

06:00	Wake up, inspection of station, breakfast
08:10	Start work, exercise
13:05	Lunch, more exercise, more work
19:30	Dinner, crew conference
21:30	Sleep

Astronauts need at least two hours of exercise each day to keep their muscles strong in the microgravity environment. They can lift weights, run on a treadmill, or use a seatless exercise bike.

Harmony

Four crew members can live in the Harmony node. Their bedrooms are tiny booths, with space for a computer and a few personal items. They sleep in a type of sleeping bag that is attached to a wall.

The bedroom also has a reading lamp, shelf, and drawer.

The Unity node is a place where all the crew can gather and eat together.

The bathroom has toothbrushes and toothpaste attached to the wall.

There is no freezer, fridge, stove, or microwave in the living quarters. Most of the food has already been cooked, then freeze-dried and vacuum-sealed.

When using the toilet, the crew must use foot straps to hold them on to the seat. The toilet uses suction, not water, to flush.

There are no chairs in the ISS!

Zvezda

There are two more sleep stations in the Zvezda module. It's possible to sleep floating freely through the station, but there is always the chance of bumping into some valuable equipment.

Working in space

Everyone on the space station stays busy. The crew has to make sure the station is in good shape, so they continually clean and check equipment, and repair or replace broken equipment. They also carry out research to advance scientific knowledge that will benefit people. This research cannot be done in the same way on Earth.

More than 200 people from 15 countries have visited and worked on the ISS. Their scientific research benefits people everywhere in their everyday lives. The results are products called spinoffs.

Space studies

Research in space helps people on Earth by:

Earth and space
- Providing a unique look at Earth and space • Improving food supplies on Earth • Studying plant biology • Studying changing glaciers, agricultural activity, forests, cities, coral reefs, and ocean currents

Meteorology
- Providing a solar observatory
- Learning about terrestrial weather, ocean currents, and science of the atmosphere
- Measuring cyclone intensity and greenhouse gases

Education

- Spreading international cooperation
- Creating the next generation of scientists
- Creating classroom materials

Human biology

- Studying humans in space in terms of balance, digestion, muscle and bone retention, heart behavior, and stress • Studying microbes, bacteria, stem cells, and tissue culture • Developing drugs to fight diseases
- Researching cancer treatments, stroke prevention, and other diseases
- Learning about crystal growth for new medicines

Physics

- Studying the building blocks of the universe, such as dark energy and dark matter
- providing astro research

Technology

- Testing robotics and telerobotics
- Advancing communication and navigation • Learning more about life support, habitation systems, and exploration destination systems
- Testing science instruments, and entry, descent, and landing systems

Dr. Bea and I had work to do in the lab. I was testing worms for medical use, while Dr. Bea was growing plants to see if microgravity affected their ability to know which way is up!

For future trips to distant planets, crews will need to be able to grow plants for a variety of uses, such as fresh vegetables for food.

Laboratory in space

Destiny is a special module that serves as a laboratory. It is attached to the main truss, or support structure, of the ISS. Hundreds of experiments can be stored and operated there.

Destiny has a freezer that is used to store samples, and to transport them to and from the space station in a temperature-controlled environment.

An astronaut inspects the Minus Eighty Laboratory Freezer in Destiny, which has a temperature of -112°F (-80°C).

Greenhouse

Growing plants in space is a challenge! Seeds don't remain in the soil in microgravity conditions, and they have a hard time knowing which way is up and down, so they often won't sprout in the right direction. Water and air in the soil also move differently.

Now there is a pop-up greenhouse to store some specially-designed grow bags on the ISS. Here, scientists can experiment with growing fresh vegetables such as lettuce.

An astronaut inspects the plants in the Destiny lab.

Crop camera

A special camera at the main observation window of Destiny takes ultraviolet images of **vegetated** areas on Earth. This information helps scientists who are concerned with agriculture. It helps them understand seasonal weather conditions on Earth and their effect on crops.

Lettuce plants are grown in a special grow bag and kept cool.

Taking a spacewalk

There is always maintenance work to do on the ISS. Checks and repairs are a regular task. Then one day, NASA warned us a problem was coming our way.

It looked as though a bombardment of meteor debris could strike the ISS and possibly damage the electronics. I joined the team on a **spacewalk** to help them get an extra shield in place.

But the meteor storm hit early and I was knocked off balance. Even worse, it broke my harness. I was no longer attached to the spacecraft! Quickly, I grabbed the control that operated the safety equipment in my backpack.

At once, it fired small jet thrusters which pushed me back to safety.

Maintenance work and repairs on the ISS mean taking a spacewalk, which is known as Extravehicular Activity, or EVA.

Two astronauts are shown working to attach a new section to the main truss of the ISS.

Around and around

The ISS is one of the most recent space stations operating in orbit around Earth. Those that went before it include the Russian Salyut, Mir, and Almaz (military observation) space stations, and the American Skylab. There is also the new Chinese Tiangong I space station.

The former Soviet Union sent up the Mir space station, which operated until 2001. It was the first space station made up of modules.

Space junk

Space may look empty from down here, but it's full of junk. A lot of satellites and other stuff have just been left up there, moving around Earth until they eventually fall into its atmosphere and burn up. NASA estimates there are 500,000 pieces of space junk orbiting Earth and they're all moving at speeds of up to 17,340 miles per hour (27,906 kph). They are a constant danger to any spacecraft with humans aboard. If a piece of space junk gets too close, NASA can move the ISS out of the way.

Salyut 7 flew in low orbit until 1991. It was the tenth space station of any kind and was visited by ten crews.

There are 500,000 pieces of space junk orbiting Earth.

Up and down

If you're aboard the ISS, 248 miles (400 km) above Earth, it's a bit difficult to go shopping. So your supplies are brought to you on the spacecraft **Dragon**.

Dragon is launched on a Falcon rocket.

Dragon is loaded with supplies and launched into space aboard a Falcon rocket. When it reaches the ISS, several rocket burns maneuver it into place. Then it's grabbed by the station's Cadadarm2 and attached to a port on the Harmony node.

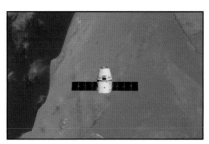

Spacecraft Dragon on its way to the ISS

On board are 1,102 pounds (500 kg) of items and provisions for the station's crew, 1,142 pounds (518 kg) of space station hardware and equipment, 35 pounds (16 kg) of computer and electronic equipment, and 112 pounds (51 kg) of hardware for spacewalks, scientific hardware and experiments for research projects—plus a new coffee maker!

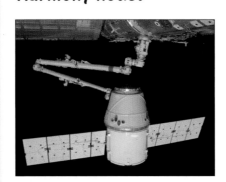

Dragon is grabbed by Canadarm2.

The Hubble Space Telescope is one of the most important items in space. It takes images of our distant universe without interference from Earth's atmosphere.

Skylab was the first American space station. It orbited from 1973 until 1979. Inside was a workshop, a solar observatory, and systems to allow the crew to spend up to 84 days in space.

Coming home

Leaving the ISS, astronauts enter the Soyuz return capsule, a cone-shaped vehicle with rocket power. This will take them back to Earth. Four parachutes open and 6 small engines fire to slow down the capsule, but it will still land with a mighty bump.

There are 7 stages to the landing:
1) The capsule enters Earth's atmosphere.
2) The hatch above the parachute flies off.
3) Two small parachutes open 15 minutes before landing.
4) A third larger parachute comes out.

5) The main parachute comes out and opens fully while the protective heat shield is cast off.

6) About 3 feet (1 meter) from the ground, 6 small engines fire to make the landing as soft as possible.

7) The ground crew is waiting to open the hatch door and help the astronauts out.

The future

The United States plans to keep the ISS working in space until 2020. With its many other international partners, it should continue the work of science research and international cooperation for years to come.

Meanwhile, NASA is using the lessons learned on the space station to prepare for human missions to places even farther into space.

NASA control center tracking the ISS

Track the ISS

There are times when you can see the space station from where you live. Visit www.jsc.nasa.gov/sightings/index.html to find out when you can see the ISS.

So Bea and I were back on Earth after an amazing three months in space. We did some useful research and were looking forward to passing our findings on to other scientists.

Who knows—maybe when astronauts travel to Mars on what will be a much longer journey, they will be nibbling on Bea's plants.

Glossary

Canadarm2
The long robotic arm that extends from the ISS truss and can help position objects

candidate
A person suitable for a job or position

Destiny
The American laboratory and research store aboard the ISS

Dragon
The small capsule used to carry goods to and from the ISS

freefall
The natural way in which an object falls back to Earth

gravity
The force that pulls all objects toward each other. It decreases as objects move farther apart.

Harmony
The living quarters of the American crew members aboard the ISS

Japanese Experiment Module
The laboratory and research module of the ISS Japanese partners

meteorology
The study of weather and climate. This is recorded in a different way from space.

microgravity
The state of reduced gravity when an object is in freefall

module
A storage or working area attached in some way to the main ISS truss

NASA
Stands for National Aeronautics and Space Administration, which is the American space agency

node
A joining section that leads from one module of the ISS to another

simulator
A machine or apparatus in which astronauts can experience a different environment

Soyuz
The Russian rocket structure that carries astronauts to and from the International Space Station

spacewalk
Any activity that takes place outside the spacecraft. Also known as an Extra Vehicular Activity or EVA.

truss
The long extended framework of the ISS, which forms the structure to which every other part is joined, either directly or indirectly

Unity
A node between the Russian and American sections of the ISS where everyone can gather

vegetated
Covered with plants or vegetation

Zvezda
The Russian service module and living quarters aboard the ISS

Learn more...

Books:

How to be a Space Explorer: Your Out-of-this-World Adventure
by Lonely Planet Kids.
Lonely Planet, 2014

Exploring Space Travel
by Laura Hamilton Waxman.
Lerner, 2013

Space Travel
by James M. Flammang.
Cherry Lake Publishing, 2013

Websites:

Learn about the parts of space and their place in the universe.
http://spaceplace.nasa.gov/menu/space/

See facts about the history of space and spacecraft.
http://easyscienceforkids.com/all-about-space-travel/

Explore space and what it's like to be an astronaut.
www.esa.int/esaKIDSen/SEMTOEBE8JG_LifeinSpace_0.html

Index